AN INTRODUCTION TO
BIRDWATCHING
Wild Wings

AN INTRODUCTION TO
BIRDWATCHING
Wild Wings

Tim Fitzharris

Text and Photographs

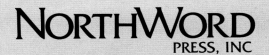

NORTHWORD
PRESS, INC

Box 1360, Minocqua, Wisconsin 54548

Turkey vultures sail over the boreal forest.

Preceding Pages: In courtship male and female lesser scaups engage in close-quarter swimming and diving manoeuvres.

Library of Congress Cataloging-in-Publication Data

Fitzharris, Tim, 1948-
    Wild Wings: an introduction to birdwatching / by Tim
Fitzharris   p.cm.
    Rev. ed. of: American birds.
    Includes bibliographical references and index.
    ISBN 1-55971-178-7: $29.95
    1. Bird watching -- North America,   2. Birds -- North
America.
I. Fitzharris, Tim. 1948-   American birds. II. Title.
QL681.F59 1992   92-8927
598' .0723473--dc20   CIP

For a free catalog describing NorthWord's line of nature books and gifts, call 1-800-336-5666.

ISBN 1-55971-178-7
Printed and bound in Singapore

To Audrey

An American white pelican yawns, revealing its expandable pouch.

American avocets gather at wintering grounds on the Gulf of Mexico. They will return to nesting territories as far north as the Canadian prairies.

Contents

Introduction

The grebe turned its head from side to side to appraise me. Eyes honed sharp by danger and the hunt and millions of years of evolution, eyes that could steer a migrating bird through a stormy night or hurtle it onto a silver sliver of fish in a swift river. The grebe paddled around me suspiciously, pumping its head up and down, sending a gentle wave curling against my camouflaged blind. Through the camera I followed its movements as unobtrusively as possible, releasing the shutter whenever I could bring the swimming bird into sharp focus. In protest, perhaps, its bill opened, setting loose a wailing song that rolled over me and into the sleeping mist. The grebe submerged until only its head and neck were visible, a vapour of feathers suspended on the surface — and then it was gone. The grebe's energy had spoken with a mysterious power. By good fortune I had recorded this elegant arrangement of life. The day and the universe seemed complete and I had yet to eat breakfast.

Photographing birds and their activities is my preoccupation. It is as much fun today as when I first began in a great blue heron rookery in Ontario in 1972, a two-year project that produced few satisfactory photographs but nourished my addiction. I enjoy birds mostly through the medium of photography. Others like to paint them, or record their songs, study their behaviour, identify and count them, feed them, band them, write about them, or just observe them. But however you come to relate to birds, in the beginning you need to develop some rudimentary birdwatching skills.

Birdwatching Basics

Birdwatching depends on the full use of the senses of sight and hearing. Birdwatchers make sure their glasses are polished and their hearing aids tuned up before heading for the woods. Most of them carry binoculars, some carry field guides, a few stuff pencils and note

An eared grebe floats motionless. By compressing feathers, grebes can submerge with scarcely a ripple.

11

pads into their pockets. The truly addicted add telescopes, cassette recorders, and small squeaking devices that imitate a variety of bird calls.

Harry, Is That a Bullfinch?

When you see a bird in North America it could be any one of about eight hundred species; to the uninitiated the variety alone is intimidating. But most people already know the names of fifty or even more species, and only a portion of the continent's total are found regularly in your area. Most birds are members of large, closely related families, and when you know the characteristics of one it becomes easy to identify others.

To get started you need a field guide —a toteable reference book that lets you look up a bird immediately while its characteristics are fresh in your mind, or even while it poses in front of you. There are many guides to choose from, but the one published by the National Geographic Society is the best, with the Golden Press version running a close second. No others are really worth considering.

You'll enjoy leafing through the field guide even when you are not outside bat-

Aided by a wingspan of almost two metres (seven feet), a northern gannet sails over its nesting colony.

tling the mosquitoes in search of new species. Find out what the biggest North American bird is, the smallest, the rarest, the most common, the greenest. Which birds have the scariest beaks, the longest, the broadest, the thinnest, the funniest? Make a list of all the birds with webbed feet. Look up all the ones whose names begin with the letter 'b'. Study the pictures and try perching like a wet cormorant or walking like a mallard.

If this sounds like fun, it is. But better yet, you will soon learn to tell whether a strange bird is a thrush or warbler, heron or crane, gull or tern. A flash of olive green in the trees will set your fingers flipping to the section on flycatchers, while a notched tail and pointed wings can only mean the swallow section, unless perhaps you are at the seashore — then it might mean tern, or if you are in Florida, it might mean swallow-tailed kite. But these refinements come easily once you have progressed this far.

Binoculars are the only other essential for birdwatching. Buy the best pair you can afford; you will be using them a lot. Most birdwatching is done with binoculars that are seven or eight power. This means that you will be observing the bird seven or eight times closer than with the naked eye. The first number in binocular specifications (7 x 28) denotes the power, the second

Beak stuffed with capelin, an Atlantic puffin prepares to feed its young hidden in a nearby burrow.

one how bright the scene will be. The larger the second number the more brilliant and clear the view, but this also means larger lens elements and more weight. Because I usually carry a lot of camera gear in the field, I opt for compact binoculars and therefore must settle for an image that is less than optimal in dark forests or twilight. Serious birdwatchers carry hefty field glasses for good reasons.

I'm Ready for the Field, Now What?

Identifying birds comes naturally to human beings; we try to identify everything we come across — a friend at the supermarket, a model of automobile, a greyhound, a blood hound, a basset hound. Birdwatching requires the same skills of observation that we have been using since birth. It's mostly a matter of familiarizing yourself with those characteristics of a bird that are helpful in cinching identification.

The most evident characteristic of a bird is its size. The easiest way to think of size is in terms of the birds you already know — hummingbirds and sparrows (small), robins and pigeons (medium), crows and hawks (large), great blue herons and swans (very large). Your field guide

Poised atop a raft of bull kelp, a great blue heron waits for fish to draw near.

14

gives measurements for all species, and you can draw comparisons based on the birds familiar to you. Unfortunately, size is a relative characteristic; you can't always tell how big a bird is, especially when it is flying in an empty sky away from trees or buildings, or is isolated in some way from other size references.

Shape is a more reliable clue to a bird's identity. Each family has a characteristic shape — herons are long-legged, long-billed, and long-necked, owls are chunky with big heads and no necks, jays have short, round wings and long tails. Plovers and sandpipers have similar shapes except for their bills: a plover's is swollen at the tip, a sandpiper's looks like a thin lance and in some species is curved. Bird shapes are obvious whether seen in a sunlit meadow or silhouetted against a full moon, and unlike sizes, they are distinctive in themselves.

You're hiking through the forest and spot a bird hammering its bill into the side of a tree. Immediately you think 'woodpecker'. On the same tree another bird is walking down the trunk headfirst, and still another inconspicuous specimen is spiralling up the trunk. The last two aren't so well known, but the chances are great that the upside-down bird is a nuthatch and the spiral climber is a brown creeper. Behaviour is a reliable and obvious clue to bird identification. Think of a robin hunting on your lawn. No other bird shares those stop-and-start rushes, those smooth rat-a-tat strides and that motionless, head-cocked pose when it is hunting night-crawlers. At first you will recognize only the behaviour of familiar birds, but if you learn to carefully observe the activities of new species, you will find it much easier to identify them on the next encounter.

The flying styles of birds vary considerably and provide easy means of identification, particularly of bird families. A flicker (like its woodpecker relatives) flies as if it were on a roller coaster, alternately flapping and swoop-gliding; a cormorant moves through the air with its body tilted as if flying uphill; a sandhill crane flaps faster on the upstroke of its wings than on the downstroke; a tern flies buoyantly, bobbing like a cork in the water with each wingbeat; turkey vultures soar with wings locked into a flat V, rocking regularly from side to side. And who could mistake the flight of a hummingbird? The sound alone gives it away.

Every game has its hard edges — hitting a knuckleball, blasting out of a sand-trap, landing on Boardwalk — and for the birdwatcher it's the *Empidonax* flycatchers, a tedious little genus with ten species, all so similar I'm sure they have trouble telling themselves apart. After careful research I discovered a small town on the west coast a couple of years ago where one is likely to encounter only four species of *Empidonax*. I immediately took residence. How the margin for error shrank. Now what joy to cast my binoculars onto one of those slim olive-drab specimens. Is it the western, the Hammond's, the dusky, or the willow? My mind dances over the narrowness of choice and then I simply pick one — and twenty-five per cent of the time I'm right! There are many easily confused species; the sparrows and warblers in particular cause birders to squint a lot and paw at their field guides. But what saves the day and fuels the addiction is that many species can be eliminated simply because their ranges lie outside the birder's territory.

Bird ranges are a birder's best friend, but you can't always trust them. The maps in your field guide are constantly under revision as new information about sightings is gathered. And of course birds make mistakes and stray outside the ranges drawn for them by ornithologists.

If you want to make birdwatching really easy, learn the preferred habitats of

An American robin broods her young. Robins show persistent alarm when humans are near their nest.

In the fog these shorebirds appear similar, but their bills distinguish them. The marbled godwits have longer, orange-tinted bills while the willets have black ones.

18

individual species from your field guide. As your experience in the field grows, you can quickly draw your own conclusions. Consider the wrens, a distinctive family of similar species, most of which are small and chunky with peppy songs and up-tilted tails. But each has a particular habitat where it is likely to be found: if you spot a wren in a farmyard or suburban neighbourhood, it's likely a house wren; the Bewick's wren is a denizen of brush and hedgerows. In fact, most of the wrens are named for their preferred habitats — cactus wren, marsh wren, sedge wren, rock wren, canyon wren. What could be easier? Using habitat to identify birds works well with many species. Of all the owls there are only two that the birdwatcher expects to see in open country — the short-eared owl and the burrowing owl — and these species give away their identity with distinctive flight patterns.

The graduating birdwatching class studies 'field marks', those telltale physical characteristics that are more readily distinguished in the little colour sketches of the field guide than they are through the binoculars. When homing in on the precise identification of a difficult species, you should pay attention to such characteristics as the shape of tail, head, and bill, the colour of legs, feet, bill, wing linings, and eyebrows, and the presence of eye rings,

wing bars, spots, streaks, tail bands, and moustaches — to cite only a partial list. Keep in mind that many of these characteristics vary seasonally and with the age of the bird.

No birdwatcher earns greater esteem than he/she who can identify the enemy by sound alone. Think of it: no need to stray into the bramble patch, no need for binoculars, no need even to look up from the morning paper. *Buzzy buzzy zip*: parula warbler in the treetops. *Teedle-eet, teedle-eet*: American tree sparrow — probably a flock of them. *Fee-bee, fee-bee-ee*: black-capped chickadee in the mood to mate.

You can learn about bird sounds from your field guide. It spells out phonetic equivalents of songs and call-notes for many species. But birds didn't learn to sing from books, and they use a completely different alphabet in real life, one that has few consonants. Consequently, what we read translates badly or sometimes not at all once we're in the forest. Another way is to listen carefully to birds while you're actually watching them. Some birds will only give you a thin, nondescript chirp or two

The dark green ear patch of the male green-winged teal is one of its distinguishing field marks.

A male song sparrow sings its courtship song. Sparrow species, similar in appearance, are often distinguished by song and behaviour.

before flying off. Others, like the red-eyed vireo, will sing steadily for an hour or more, making their songs easy to study. Unfortunately, on a spring morning you're likely to suffer acoustic overload, especially if you're birding in a forest. The number of birds you hear will be three or four times greater than the number you actually see.

The most effective way to learn bird songs is to listen to recordings made in the field and produced commercially as cassette tapes or discs. The best ones are made by the Cornell University Laboratory of Ornithology and published by the Houghton Mifflin Company. Difficult songs can be played repeatedly, and those that are similar and easily confused can be readily compared. This kind of advance preparation will add great excitement to your birding forays, especially if you study the birds in groups according to habitat. Warming up with a few quick recordings of songbirds of the Carolinian forest, for example, just prior to an expedition, will give you a psychological advantage over the birds and a leg up on your birding friends.

No matter how much I listen to bird songs I can't remember them for very long. They don't sink in. If you should have the same problem, try what a lot of ornithologists do when they're on sabbatical. They write lyrics for bird melodies — actual words and sentences that birds would use if they could talk instead of just whistle. Here are a few of the more famous results: *Drink your tea!* (rufous-sided towhee), *Old Sam Peabody Peabody Peabody!* (white-throated sparrow), *Teacher Teacher Teacher!* (ovenbird), *Sweet Sweet Sweeter than Sweet!* (yellow warbler), *Quick Three Beers!* (olive-sided flycatcher), and, last of all, my favourite, *Pizza!* (Acadian flycatcher). But you are as qualified as anyone to put words into the beaks of birds. It's not necessary to use existing ones if others more poignant and memorable occur to you. Listen to the recordings and write your own words. The next time you're in the field you'll discover that the birds are singing your song.

A few final suggestions for your field excursions. First the bad news: dedicated birders start out before dawn. But don't worry: your head will clear with the sight of the first barn owl you spot winging back to its roost, or geese migrating in the twilight. The most productive birding is found in marginal habitats — areas where forest intergrades with meadow or meadow with brushland, where marsh borders on desert. Such habitats have a diversity of feeding, nesting, and roosting opportunities and are consequently attractive to many birds. Move in a relaxed, casual manner. Talk

Early morning sees the gathering of an immature bald eagle, crow, and waterfowl on the West Coast.

22

Preceding Pages: Most North American birders must travel a long way to record the great white heron, a subspecies of the great blue heron that is found only in southern Florida.

quietly or try a few bird song imitations. Make a *pishh*ing sound to bring small perching birds out of the underbrush. Don't sneak up on birds. They'll spook and head for cover when they inevitably spot you. They'll tell other birds that you were trying to eat them. Last of all, remember that the reason we don't consider birds to be intelligent is that we aren't smart enough to figure out what they think about.

Doctor, I've Got This Problem with Birds

By the time you've put all these suggestions into practice you'll be ready for some real birding. For most enthusiasts this means, at the very least, keeping a life list — a written account of every new bird species you see, usually by name, place, and date. Some people really become enthused about their life list, hopping on jets to fly across the continent to get a look at a bird that has strayed in from Europe or Asia. The true fanatics taxi directly from the airport to the bird, make visual contact, and taxi right back to the airport.

There are many variations on the list theme — yearly lists, monthly lists, vacation lists, backyard lists. One of the most interesting is the 'big day' list. This is the

In a city park a mallard hen and wood duck drake study the photographer.

product of a fast moving exercise, often carried out by teams, to spot as many species as possible in a single day. Keen competitors carefully plan the itinerary to cover as many habitats as possible. They start out just after midnight, drink gallons of stale black coffee, speed along congested freeways between marsh, seashore, and forest, and at the end of the day they may have up to a hundred and fifty species on their list.

Birdwatching also means studying the behaviour of visitors to backyard feeders, observing ducks in the city park, or sitting quietly in a forest or meadow while thrushes and sparrows forage almost at arm's length. Many birdwatchers become involved with conservation organizations that work for the welfare of birds. These societies are primarily concerned with developing a better understanding of birds and raising public awareness of birds, nature, and environmental issues generally.

Meadow and Prairie

Meadow and Prairie

Most of North America's grasslands are found west of the Great Lakes in areas where there is too little rainfall to support the growth of trees. This region is extensively planted with grains; in the drier areas ranches are common and cattle have replaced the once immense herds of buffalo and pronghorn. In eastern North America much of the original forest was cleared by the early settlers, and today this land is farmed or developed for industrial and residential purposes. Here and there, however, fields are left fallow or used for grazing livestock, allowing more natural meadows to develop.

For the birdwatcher grasslands and meadows offer uninterrupted viewing, making birds easier to spot but generally more wary of approach than those of the forest. Many species found here are exuberant singers, with powerful voices that carry over the often windswept terrain. With few natural perches, courtship rituals and songs may be performed on the wing. Because there is little cover beyond grasses and herbs, camouflaged plumages are necessary here, and when threatened most species freeze, thereby disappearing into the vegetation. With few reasons to leave the ground, many birds — larks, cranes, grouse, and quail — have evolved strong legs and feet for running. Ground nesters are common, and they often have precocious young that are able to follow after their parents the same day they hatch, making them less vulnerable to predators.

Birdwatching in open, grassy areas calls for powerful binoculars. It also helps to be familiar with the songs of typical species, as well as their silhouettes and behavioural characteristics. The bubbling, flute-like melodies of the western meadowlark, the spread of a golden eagle's wings against a blue sky, an American kestrel hovering over a pasture as it scans for insects, the grasshopper sparrow's short flight-dives into the grass when it is flushed out, and the raised wings of an upland sandpiper as it alights are but a few of the sights and sounds that could appear in your grassland field notes.

One of the largest birds of the prairie, a sandhill crane emits a loud, gargling call.

Of North America's three bluebird species, the eastern bluebird, an inhabitant of meadows, orchards, and parks, is the most familiar. It is distinguished from the mountain bluebird by its orange breast and from the western bluebird by its orange throat. An early migrant in the northern part of its range, the eastern bluebird arrives on the breeding grounds when snow still lingers, announcing with a musical *chur chur-lee chur-lee* the onset of spring. Eastern bluebirds are cavity-nesters, and their early appearance on breeding territories allows them first opportunity to occupy sites also sought by house wrens, tree swallows, flickers, and flying squirrels.

The introduction of stronger, more aggressive, non-migratory European starlings and house sparrows in the last century ended the bluebird's advantage. At the same time the bluebird was losing nest sites to these introduced species, its food supply — primarily insects — was being destroyed by the use of agricultural pesticides. Today bluebird numbers are rising as a result of concerted public efforts to provide artificial nesting boxes.

A male eastern bluebird has just passed an insect to his mate.

The plumage of the female eastern bluebird is paler than the male's.

The piercing *kill-dee, kill-dee* call of the killdeer is heard throughout North America except in far northern regions. Identified by double black breast bands, this compact bird can be seen on farm fields, lawns, and river banks — darting, stopping, and darting off again atop a blur of churning legs. Primarily a forager of insects and larvae, the killdeer often follows farmers ploughing their fields, plucking grubs churned up in the furrows.

It nests on open ground, preferring to lay its three to five eggs among stones or gravel where their grey, mottled pattern is effective camouflage. Adults fly in the face of approaching livestock to protect their eggs from trampling and are famous for the broken-wing routine used to lure predators away from the nest site. Sometimes killdeers nest on gravel rooftops up to five storeys high; once their feathers are dry, the newly hatched young follow their parents to the edge and flutter to the ground unharmed.

A killdeer distracts predators from its nesting site.

The most numerous and familiar birds belong to the order *Passeriformes* or perching birds. With strong, flexible toes, three pointing forward and one backward, all at the tip of the foot, these birds are able to grasp firmly branches, twigs, and, in the case of the smallest species, even grass. With a wingspan of over a metre (three and a half feet), the raven is the largest perching bird. It is six times longer and more than two hundred times heavier than one of smallest, the golden-crowned kinglet. For most perching birds song is important in communication and courtship.

Like many birds that breed in meadows and grasslands, the bobolink effectively broadcasts its territorial claims even in the frequently windy conditions of its open habitat, with a bubbling, tinkling song, often given in flight. After migrating 8000 kilometres (5000 miles) from its wintering grounds, the pampas of southern Brazil and northern Argentina, the female bobolink is seduced by the male's spirited courting and joins his harem. She hides her nest on the ground in a dense patch of grass and lays four to seven eggs in late spring or early summer. The male assists his mates in feeding the young. Bobolinks were abundant in the last century, descending to feed in the millions on rice fields in the southern United States as they returned to South America. Even though they weigh only forty grams (one ounce), they were numerous enough to merit commercial harvesting, and thousands were sold in eastern cities.

A female bobolink rests momentarily in a grassy meadow. Like all perching birds, she has toes adapted for holding onto stems and twigs.

Over thirty species of sparrows are found in North America. All are small, brown birds that feed on or near the ground, usually in flocks except during the nesting season. Important clues to identification are derived from head and breast pattern, behaviour, habitat, and song.

The savannah sparrow's best field marks are the yellow streak over each eye, the streaked breast, and the notched tail. Variations within the species and the loss of distinctive plumage patterns outside the nesting season may make it resemble other species with overlapping ranges. In such circumstances a knowledge of the savannah sparrow's call notes and its flushing, feeding, and flocking behaviour may be needed for identification.

Whereas the savannah sparrow prefers large fields with short grass, its relative, the song sparrow, frequents open brushy habitat. A springtime visit to such terrain in the northern half of the United States and Canada (except for the Arctic) confirms this species' scientific name: *Melospiza melodia* (song finch with a pleasing song). The male serenades repeatedly with a series of short, bright notes ending with a distinctive trill.

Although highly variable in plumage, most savannah sparrows have a distinctive yellow line over the eye.

38

A male song sparrow alights on its singing perch from which it broadcasts territorial claims.

The largest members of the shorebird family, the marbled godwit and the long-billed curlew once migrated in huge flocks along the eastern seaboard. In their abundance they were slaughtered by hunters unable to foresee the day when the sighting of even a single bird would be an exciting event for eastern birdwatchers. Today both species are protected. On western meadows godwits still spring into the air on sighting an intruder, swooping overhead bombarding the trespasser with a clamour of alarm calls at each pass. Hatchling curlews run stilt-legged in the shadows of their mothers, snapping insects from the tangle of grass with bills that quickly develop into slender, down-curving pincers up to twenty centimetres (eight inches) long. Even though both shorebirds are fairly common in the west, their numbers continue to decline because of the gradual loss of meadow and prairie nesting habitat and the decline of wetlands and natural shorelines where both species feed, especially during migration.

A marbled godwit bathes in a prairie slough.

The long-billed curlew uses its slender bill to probe for
worms and catch frogs, grasshoppers, spiders, and
even flying insects.

Before dawn on a small patch of sagebrush, a strange plopping sound intrudes on the spring silence — a male sage grouse engrossed in his courtship display. The plain begins to bubble and pop as nearby cocks join in until more than a hundred are courting simultaneously. The noisy display of spread feathers and bulging yellow air sacs continues for several hours as each cock seeks to win a hen.

The sage grouse is by far the largest North American grouse. It is aptly named, for its plumage is patterned to blend with the sagebrush, it eats the leaves and shoots of sagebrush, it builds its nest under sagebrush, and it roosts among these plants during harsh weather.

The territorial claim of the ring-necked pheasant (next page) is also strange — a crowing screech that sounds like someone stepping onto a barbed-wire fence, followed by a deep fluttering of wings. This large, flashy game bird, introduced from Asia, is found in many parts of southern Canada and much of the United States. When flushed it rises almost vertically on short churning wings, croaking hoarsely, its large mottled body and streamer tail sailing heavily toward the nearest hedgerow or woodlot.

On the breeding grounds, male sage grouse shake and inflate their air sacs and spread their tail feathers.

A cock ring-necked pheasant shows his red eye patches, snowy neck ring, and iridescent ear tufts.

The slow, direct flight of the ring-necked pheasant makes it easy prey for a gyrfalcon. Breeding in the Arctic, these large falcons move south during the winter, appearing on seashores, lake sides, and prairies.

Owls are the night-time counterparts of the hawks and falcons. All have keen, immobile eyes set in large, swivelling heads. Their feathers are soft and fluffy, making flight almost soundless. Owls' hearing is extremely acute, and some species are able to capture their prey in complete darkness.

The burrowing owl lives in grasslands and other open, dry habitats, particularly where rodent burrows are numerous. About the size of a robin, it has long, spindly legs and a short tail. Its call, a soft, mournful *coo-cooo*, is heard once the sun sets. The burrowing owl begins hunting at twilight, hovering frequently as it scours the ground for small rodents, beetles, and crickets; dragonflies, moths, and even bats

A pair of burrowing owls stand near their nesting hole.

are snatched from mid-air. The owl lays up to nine eggs in an old ground squirrel burrow. When sufficiently large, the rapidly growing young stand around on the entrance mound during the day. If a predator threatens they file below, giving a distress call that mimics the warning of a rattlesnake.

Unlike the burrowing owl, which is primarily a bird of western North America, the short-eared owl is found in open country throughout most of the continent including the low Arctic. It is active during the day, flying a wavering course on erratic wingbeats — a characteristic that makes identification easy, even at a distance. Often the objects of these daylight forays are small birds, although the short-eared owl subsists mainly on mice. It nests on the ground in tall grass or even marsh vegetation.

A short-eared owl hunts rodents from a fence post.

49

The ferruginous hawk belongs to a large group of soaring hawks called *buteos* — birds of prey with broad, banded tails and large, rounded wings. It inhabits the dry plains, canyons, and badlands of the west where it is often sighted gliding with still, spread wings high on thermal air currents. The ferruginous prefers to nest in trees but commonly builds its bulky structures on the ground near a canyon precipice or on a rock outcrop of a coulee. Made of sticks, old bones, dried grass, and cow dung, the nest is added to each year, sometimes attaining a depth of four metres (thirteen feet). The frequently vulnerable location of the nest makes the ferruginous an aggressive defender of its territory, and it will drive off foxes, great-horned owls, and even coyotes that venture too near. It eats mice, jackrabbits, prairie dogs, and especially ground squirrels, using a variety of techniques — hunting from atop a fence post or pole, coursing low over the ground, or hovering at higher altitudes.

Protective of its young, a ferruginous hawk screams an alarm. It can drive away predators as large as coyotes from the nest.

In April small flocks of sandhill cranes appear over the prairies. Buoyed by thermal air currents, the great birds (wingspan 2 m./6.6 ft.) spiral slowly northward at high altitudes. At day's end they alight in a marsh or stubble field to feed and rest. Courtship may also be carried out, the lanky cranes springing upward on outstretched wings while their powerful gurgling songs reverberate over the flat land. Some birds remain on the prairies to nest, while others continue on to the marshes and muskegs of the tundra. Once on the breeding grounds the crane takes about three months to incubate the eggs and nourish the young to flying size. In September long skeins of cranes appear again over the ripening grainfields, now bound for their wintering grounds in California and Central America.

Sandhill cranes migrate over the prairie.

Marsh and Lake

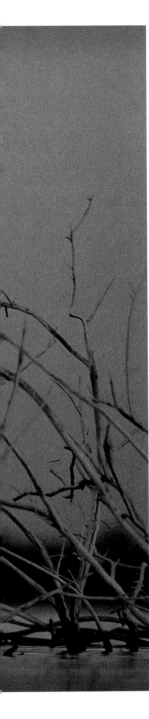

Marsh and Lake

Small, shallow bodies of water have the most abundant bird life. Such conditions permit sunlight and carbon dioxide to enter the water and favour the growth of aquatic vegetation (pondweeds, algae). The shoreline area is large in relation to the amount of open water, and emergent vegetation (cattails, bulrushes, sedges) proliferates. This plant community supports a diverse community of animals, including birds and the organisms they prey on.

Waterbirds have many adaptations for their habitat. To stay dry they have large glands that secrete oil, which is spread through the feathers with bill or feet. Birds commonly have light, honey-combed bones for ease of flying, but water birds have solid, heavy bones for diving underwater. Many have short legs, and their toes are webbed or lobed for swimming. Others have long, thin legs to keep their bodies dry when they are wading in the shallows, or spreading toes to support them on soft mud or lily pads. The bills of some ducks and flamingoes are lined with strainers to sift small animals and seeds from the water. The serrated bills of mergansers hold on to squirming fish; the lance-shaped bills of herons can stab quickly into the water after fish or frogs. Shorebirds have tubular bills with sensitive tips for probing soft bottoms or exposed mudflats. Water birds are migratory and often fly long distances to reach open water when ice seals off their breeding territories.

When birding in lakes and marshes, it's helpful to wear rubber boots or even hip waders to work your way around the shoreline. As in other habitats, early morning provides the most activity, and migration in the spring and fall brings birds that normally reside thousands of miles away into your region—a great way to increase your life list. On large lakes, powerful binoculars or even a spotting scope come in handy for puzzling out ducks, loons, or grebes rafting far from shore. Brush up on the silhouettes of flying water birds, especially the flashing wing patterns of ducks, which are identifiable at long range.

Black-crowned night herons perch on dead trees above a marsh.

The herons are one of the best-known bird families in North America. Their large size and lanky bodies, adapted for wading in shallow water as they hunt for aquatic animals, make them conspicuous and easy to recognize. Unlike other long-legged wading birds, which fly with necks outstretched, herons fly with their necks curled against the breast. All members of the heron family develop a characteristic type of feather called 'powder down' that grows continuously and frays at the tip, producing a powder that the birds use to clean their plumage.

Black-crowned night herons are squat, crow-sized members of the heron family. During the day they roost in dense thickets, remaining concealed until just before sunset when they fly out to the feeding grounds to fish.

The largest North American heron is the great blue. More than a metre (three and a half feet) tall, it is often observed standing statue-like in the shallows of a marsh or lake. Its long neck stretches out over the still water as its keen eyes scan the depths for a fish, frog, or crayfish. From time to time the heron moves to a new position on reed-like legs that cause scarcely a ripple. Suddenly it strikes, the slim head shattering the mirrored surface. The heron pulls a squirming victim from the water, shakes it vigorously, and then swallows it headfirst. Large prey may continue to struggle as it moves through the long esophagus, causing the heron's neck to bulge and twitch.

If startled during its hunting, the great blue issues an abrupt series of alarm croaks and springs from the tangle of cattails or bulrushes, its broad wings flapping heavily as it disappears, protesting noisily.

The white hindneck plumes of the black-crowned night heron are longest during the breeding season.

Preceding Pages: Before swallowing, a great blue heron flips a fish to prevent spiny fins from harming its throat.

Like other herons, the snowy egret has luxurious feathers and sweeping plumes that once made it the target of hunters who supplied the millinery trade. Luckily fashion gave way to conservation, and the numbers of this dainty heron recovered. The snowy egret hunts the shallows energetically, seldom pausing as it rushes here and there, occasionally stirring up the bottom with its feet and stabbing continually into the water after small prey. Once in a while it lifts a long leg clear of the water, revealing its yellow toes and the reason for its nickname 'golden slippers'.

In contrast to the snowy egret, its relative the American bittern is known for being secretive. The bittern is seldom found away from a stand of bulrushes or cattails, and if threatened points its bill to the sky, extends its long, striped neck, and amazingly disappears into its reedy surroundings. Thus camouflaged it remains frozen. If the wind is blowing the bittern sways in concert with the stems, sustaining its ruse until the danger passes. If relaxed and intent on nesting, however, the bittern sets the marsh alive with its bizarre song —a mechanical, full-bodied melody that sounds like a thirsty water pump and has earned this heron the nickname of 'thunder pumper'. Common in wetlands throughout most of North America, the bittern will announce its presence to anyone who visits a springtime marsh after dark.

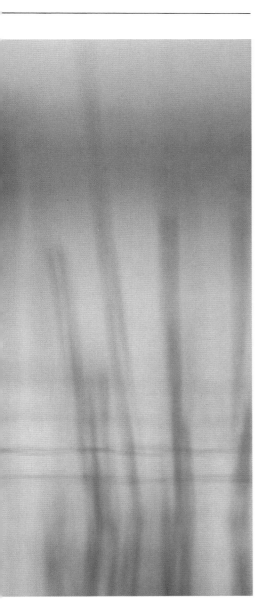

The streaked plumage of the American bittern is camouflaged to blend with marsh vegetation.

A snowy egret hunts the shallow waters of a marsh.

Many species of birds are adapted to feed in the soft mud bordering the shores of lakes and marshes. Most of them have long legs, to keep their bodies out of the water, and long, slender bills to probe for worms and other invertebrate life. Among the shorebirds that are also good swimmers are the phalaropes. Small webs and lobes on their toes assist their aquatic activities. When not patrolling the mudflats, phalaropes are likely to be found in deep water chasing surface insects, which they pluck up while swimming in tight circles.

Like all phalaropes, the Wilson's reverses the usual role of the sexes. Not only is the female larger and more brightly patterned than the male, but she takes the initiative in courtship, while her mate builds the nest, incubates the eggs, and cares for the young.

Another specialized shorebird, the avocet is equipped with long, spindly legs that permit it to feed over wide areas of the shallow prairie sloughs where it is most abundant. Unlike most shorebirds, the avocet has a long, upward-curving bill that allows it to sweep effectively through the surface slime or bottom ooze. With rhythmic back and forth movements of its lowered head, it strides through the shallows catching insects, shrimps, larvae, and small aquatic plants in its partially opened bill. Avocets are gregarious birds, feeding together in flocks of twenty or more and nesting in loose colonies. Sometimes two females will share the same nest, helping one another with incubation duties.

Unlike most birds, the female Wilson's phalarope is larger and more colourful than her mate (in the background).

An American avocet concludes a session of preening with a stretch.

Since the long-billed dowitcher nests in the Arctic and passes the winter in Central America or in the extreme south and west of the United States, most birdwatchers have a chance to view it only during migration. A chunky, medium-sized shorebird with pale eyebrows, it travels with other dowitchers in compact flocks whether on the ground or flying about the marsh, and rarely mingles with other species. Unlike the common snipe, a similar long-billed shorebird that usually feeds near or within sedges or other marsh vegetation, the dowitcher prefers open mudflats.

The long-billed dowitcher feeds in shallow water, probing the mud, often with its head under the water. Its bill is remarkable not only for its length but also for its sensitivity and flexibility. Lined with nerves, it enables the dowitcher to distinguish food buried in the mud, usually insect larvae, and the dextrous tip can open to seize prey.

Long-billed dowitchers probe the mud for small invertebrates with their sensitive bills.

The gurgling, liquid *konk-la-reeee* of the red-winged blackbird rates as the theme song of the marsh. Redwings are to be found at some time of the year throughout most of North America, but are most exciting on their nesting grounds—the marshes of the northern United States and Canada.

Atop a cattail in early spring, the male spreads his wings to display red shoulder patches and announces his territorial claims (averaging one quarter acre) to other males in the vicinity. The males carry on this vocal sparring, occasionally chasing or being chased, as the boundaries are settled. In a few weeks the females arrive in small groups, perching in the trees about the marsh to evaluate the males' displays. If impressed, they enter a territory to be claimed and courted. The male generally serves three females at the same time, although the families develop at staggered intervals, each being at a different stage of the nesting cycle. The pair bonds end once the young are able to fend for themselves, and for the rest of the year redwings remain in sexually segregated flocks.

A male red-winged blackbird spreads his wings, exposing red epaulets—behaviour that establishes territory.

The female red-winged blackbird spends much of her time building a nest and raising her young.

Although the swamp sparrow spends the non-breeding season with flocks of other sparrows, often in upland weed fields and brushy habitat, when spring arrives it heads for a marsh, swamp, or lakeshore. Here in a bush or clump of cattails it builds a cup-shaped nest of stalks, leaves, and coarse grass with a lining of finer grasses. Four or five pale-blue speckled eggs are laid and, warmed by the female alone, they hatch in about two weeks. The young are fed by the parents for another two weeks until they can flutter weakly into the surrounding vegetation, where they will continue to receive food—provided they are not eaten by bullfrogs, fish, or turtles— until they are able to hunt.

Another small songbird of cattail marshes that one hears before seeing it is the marsh wren. Males arrive on territory before the females and sing for much of the day, sometimes as often as fifteen to twenty times per minute. Once in a while a male will launch himself upward and flutter slowly down, giving song as he descends to another perch. In addition to singing, the male also builds nests, often several of them, but only the coarse outer structure.

A long-billed marsh wren fluffs outs its breast and sings its territorial claims.

When the female arrives she visits the nests while the male fluffs himself up and enthusiastically serenades her inspections. If all is satisfactory, she adds an inner layer of fine grasses to one of the nests and lays her eggs.

A swamp sparrow alights near its nest with an insect for its offspring.

Ducks are the birds most frequently associated with lakes and marshes. They belong to the family *Anatidae*, whose members are characterized by short legs and webbed toes, a long neck, and a broad bill. Unlike their close relatives the geese and swans, ducks moult twice each year (rather than once), they find a new mate every nesting season (geese and swans generally mate for life), and only the female cares for the young. But the most obvious dissimilarity is that male and female ducks of most species are strikingly different, the male being more brilliantly patterned, whereas in their larger cousins the sexes are practically indistinguishable.

One group of ducks found on inland waters are called bay ducks. They typically dive beneath the water to feed, and when they take off they must run along the surface of the water to become airborne. The redhead is a common bay duck found through much of the settled regions of North America. Aside from his fiery feathers, the male's most impressive trait is his courtship song, a bizarre, drawn-out groan that begins with the bird's neck and head thrown back to nearly touch the rump. Redhead drakes are aggressive during the breeding season, rushing across the marsh to drive away rivals.

Another common bay duck is the ring-necked. The reason for its name is usually difficult to detect in the field, as the cinnamon-hued collar blends so well into the glossy purple feathers that cover the head and neck. Readily observed, however, are the rings on the bill: two for the male and one for the female.

Following Pages: A pair of ring-necked ducks court on a northern lake.

In spring the normally silent redhead drake becomes vocal and aggressive in his pursuit of a mate.

The northern shoveler belongs to another group of ducks known as dabblers, so called for their habit of plucking small plants and animals from the surface of the water as they paddle about. Dabbling ducks also feed by 'tipping up' in shallow water, leaving only their tails visible as they stretch their bills towards the bottom. The shoveler's distinctive spatula-shaped bill is lined with comb-like projections that allow it to sift duckweed, insects, snails, worms, shrimps, small fish, and many other more minute organisms from the mud or water. The tongue and mouth are well supplied with nerves to help the shoveler distinguish its food. Shovelers sometimes team up in groups of three or four, swimming in a circular pattern so that each duck can feed on the food stirred up by the feet of the duck in front.

Like other dabblers, the shoveler has no need of a running take-off, and is able to spring directly out of the water should a fox, mink, or bobcat surprise it.

The fringes of the shoveler's bill sift small aquatic plants and animals from the mud and water.

With a powerful thrust of wings and webbed feet, a female northern shoveler launches from a prairie marsh.

The lesser scaup swims strongly underwater, using its feet and keeping its wings held tightly against its body. It feeds below the surface on insects, small molluscs, and crustaceans, and the seeds of wild rice, widgeon grass, and pondweed. It prefers water about two metres (seven feet) deep and often heads straight for the bottom to sift through the ooze. Feeding in this way, scaups are frequently poisoned by lead shot discharged by hunters.

Although lesser scaups return to their breeding grounds in Canada and the northern states in early spring, nesting activity is usually delayed until June. Many of the later nests, built on the ground near water, are destroyed by haying operations that begin in early July. The successful hens, however, hatch about twelve eggs and immediately lead these downy young to the lake where they may join other scaup families, grouping their offspring together to form rafts of up to a hundred ducklings, which are cared for co-operatively by all the hens.

The lesser scaup is popularly known as the 'bluebill'.

The drab plumage of the female lesser scaup matches that of her young, which helps conceal them from predators.

83

Species of ducks adapted to swim underwater and catch fish are called mergansers. In addition to the anatomical adaptations for swimming shared with other diving ducks, mergansers have long, serrated bills (sawbills) that help them hold onto slippery prey.

The common merganser is the largest of North America's three merganser species, being about the size of a mallard. Harbingers of spring, green-headed drakes appear over icy lakes and rivers in late winter searching for a patch of open water where they can land and fish. They prey mostly on coarse, slow-moving species such as carp, sticklebacks, sculpin, eels, and suckers. Once it snares a meal the merganser surfaces and adjusts its hold on the fish — which is often thicker than the merganser's neck — in order to swallow it headfirst. This excites the rest of the flock, which gathers around in hopes of stealing the catch. Often the first owner loses the prize to another, and it then joins in the harassment. Eventually, however, the fish is swallowed and the lucky bird rests on the surface, digesting its meal and sipping water while the flock resumes hunting.

A female common merganser clears her wings of water. Feather care is an important and time-consuming activity for water birds.

The bill of the common merganser is serrated and hooked for catching fish.

Each spring and fall, ragged, undulating Vs of Canada geese move across the sky, so high at times that they might go unnoticed were it not for the honking chatter that filters to the ground. The flocks are made up of family groups consisting of goose, gander, and offspring. The young geese follow their parents south for the winter and remain with them until they return to the breeding grounds the next spring. This close-knit family behaviour, together with a tendency to nest near the spot where they were hatched, limits interbreeding of birds from diverse regions and results in significant variations within the species: as many as twenty subspecies are recognized. Although they all wear the black head stockings and white cheek patches typical of Canada geese, they vary significantly in body proportion, voice, and size; the smallest are short-necked, cackle-voiced specimens one-tenth the weight of the largest, deep-honking giants.

Canada geese seem to have benefitted from the spread of agriculture across North America, tender grasses and grains being a preferred food. In addition, the establishment of special sanctuaries for breeding, over-wintering, and resting during migration have allowed the population to soar in recent decades.

Canada geese remain paired for as long as both live.

Canada geese land in a corn field during fall migration.

Seven species of grebes are found in North America, varying in size and form from the graceful, swan-like western grebe (length 64 cm/25 in.) to the drab and stubby least grebe (length 25 cm/10 in.). Grebes nevertheless share many characteristics. Adapted to an aquatic existence, they have short, powerful legs and large lobed toes for swimming swiftly underwater. All of their activities — feeding, sleeping, and even nesting — take place on the water.

Each species carries out an elaborate courtship, a distinctive repertoire of song and swimming. Although grebes are quiet most of the year, the nesting ground resounds with an assortment of brays, trills, chuckles, wails, and whinnies as the birds dance and glide, sometimes in tandem, across the surface. Once these intricate preliminaries have had their effect, the eggs are laid in a soggy floating nest, often hidden among cattails or bulrushes. After hatching the chicks are ferried about the marsh tucked into the feathers of the parents' backs until they can swim strongly on their own.

Unable to take off from land, grebes must stay in flight until they reach another body of water. In late autumn grebes are sometimes found on iced-over lakes where they have set down in error. Here they succumb either to starvation and cold or to hungry coyotes, foxes, or hawks. Despite this apparent handicap, grebes migrate long distances, and when winter arrives in Canada most are cruising about the warmer coastal waters of the United States and Central America.

Water slides off an eared grebe's well-oiled plumage as it climbs onto its floating nest.

Following Pages: The plumage of male and female western grebes is identical–a characteristic common to all grebes.

The common loon breeds wherever there are lakes deep enough for it to dive beyond the reach of predators and broad enough to accommodate its laborious take-off, a long, wing-beating, foot-slapping run across the water. The loon is perhaps more specialized for aquatic life than any other bird. The bones of its legs and feet are far to the rear, confined within the muscles of the body; only the webbed toes extend flipper-like into the water. These limbs allow the loon to pursue the swiftest fish to depths up to sixty metres (two hundred feet). On land it is almost helpless, scooting about on its belly like a seal, unable to take off. It comes onto land only to nest and chooses a site that is a quick wiggle from the water. Unlike the air-filled bones of most birds, the loon's are solid and heavy, giving it a specific gravity close to that of water. By compressing its feathers to force out air, it can submerge with scarcely a ripple, its thick neck and head scanning the lake like a periscope before it disappears. Although loon flight is swift, it is without grace or agility — merely transportation between the loon's ancestral nesting territory inland and the coastal wintering ground.

The song of the loon is the anthem of the North American wilderness; clear, penetrating notes that echo over spruce

and birch-lined lakes every spring and summer in a repertoire of yodels, wails, and haunting laughter. A music millions of years old, its volume has decreased steadily over the past century. Loons were shot for sport, for competing for fish stocks, for meat and feathers. They continue to be driven from nesting territories by boaters and fishermen, and even now they are being killed by oil spills in their wintering areas, poisoned by toxic pollutants in their food chain, and starved because of the effects of acid rain on their lakes.

A common loon sounds its tremolo call.

A large bird of prey, the osprey inhabits forested regions near water. Its unique feet are adapted for fishing: the toes are covered with tiny spikes on the under surface and the outer ones are double-jointed, allowing the bird to strike with two toes forward and two backward. Both adaptations make it difficult for a fish to twist free once caught. The osprey usually watches over its favourite fishing holes from atop a dead snag. Sighting prey, it sails out above the victim, hovers momentarily, and then dives, talons and beak foremost, splattering the water with a momentum that carries the bird below the surface. It soon emerges on heavy wings, and if lucky, with a wiggling fish in its talons. The osprey quickly shifts its quarry around so that the head points forward to reduce wind resistance.

The osprey's nest is a massive accumulation of sticks and debris. To gather material it plummets onto a protruding branch, latches on with its talons, and allows its weight to crack off the wood. Often the osprey returns to the nest with unwieldy branches up to two metres (seven feet) long which it jams into the nest, scraping and clunking its nervous chicks.

A young osprey is fed fish by its parent.

An osprey brings in new nest material.

Woodland and Forest

Woodland and Forest

In North America deciduous forests are found in the east and coniferous types in the west and north. The more varied vegetation of the deciduous forests creates more diversity of food and reproductive habitat, which in turn supports more bird species. Common trees are oak, maple, beech, hickory, elm, and ash. Unlike the deciduous trees, which are bare in winter, the spruces, firs, pines, hemlocks, and cedars of the coniferous forests provide shelter for birds year round. Much of the continent is covered with thickets and regrowing forests — more open habitats with birds common to both grassland and forest.

During the warm seasons perching birds feed on insects and their larvae, hunting along limbs and through the foliage, or probing into bark. Migratory species like warblers and flycatchers have thin bills ideal for this task, but in the fall this specialization forces them south in search of dependable food supplies. The thicker, all-purpose bills of year round species such as the jays and crows allow them to feed on nuts, seeds, fruits, and buds when the insect supply runs out. Many warblers exploit only certain strata of the forest: the oven bird builds its domed nest right on the ground, the American redstart zips about the understorey pursuing flying insects, and the blackburnian warbler forages in the sunlit canopy. Limited visibility makes bird songs and calls important for establishing territories and keeping families together during the nesting season.

In the forest you often have only seconds to train your binoculars on a bird before it disappears. Practice at home in spotting small targets quickly will improve your chances in the field. Close-focusing binoculars (three metres/ten feet or less) are useful for birds like wrens, gnatcatchers, and warblers, which are too small to identify with the naked eye even at close range. Staying immobile with your back to a tree for ten minutes or longer is a good strategy for spotting birds that normally remain hidden and inactive while you are moving past them.

A red-tailed hawk perches on a dead tree.

With fanned tail glowing orange-red against the sun, wings spread, and an angry, plaintive cry the red-tailed hawk soars above the fields and forests of North America. The best-known and most common of our birds of prey, the red-tail builds its bulky stick nest five to twenty-five metres (sixteen to eighty feet) up in the crotch of a large tree. It prefers sites on the edge of a forest where it can hunt nearby meadows for mice and ground squirrels.

About the size of a crow, the broad-winged hawk is the red-tail's smallest relative, and has the same broad wings and tail that characterize the *buteos* (soaring hawks). Apart from its size, its best distinguishing marks are its black and white tail bands and the thin descending whistle heard in the vicinity of the nest. The broad-wing seldom strays into open country except during migration, when thousands may be seen in a single day, spiralling slowly along on rising air currents. When hunting it perches low in the forest, often near a pond or small lake, keen eyes searching for frogs, snakes, small rodents, dragonflies, or even crayfish.

A broad-winged hawk arrives at the nest to feed its downy chicks.

A red-tailed hawk feeds on an American coot.

Cheer up, cheeriup, cheerio — the American robin's loud, liquid melody does just what it professes, especially in the northern parts of its breeding range, where its early morning carolling signals the end of winter. This large thrush of woodlands and suburbs ranges throughout North America except the high Arctic. Its numbers have benefitted from residential sprawl, neatly cut lawns providing a good source of earthworms that, along with berries, fruits, and insects, comprise its diet.

The males arrive at their nesting territory before the females, and are distinguished by their darker heads and fatter, deeper orange breasts. The nest is a bulky mass of twigs, grass, string, and other odd scraps with a smooth inner cup of mud lined with fine, dry grass. The female usually lays four glossy light-blue eggs. On leaving the nest the spot-breasted young follow after their father begging for food, while the female sets about nesting again. Robins commonly raise two broods, and sometimes more, each year.

An American robin prepares to swallow a mountain ash berry, an important winter fruit for many songbirds.

The bass drummer of the deep woods, the pileated woodpecker is the largest woodpecker commonly seen in North America. Its slow, resounding hammering usually means that the pileated is chopping into a trunk or rotted stump for its dinner, often carpenter ants or wood-boring beetles. Like other woodpeckers, the pileated is well adapted for extracting its food from trees. Its brain is protected by a thick skull and a thin cushion of shock-absorbing air; it has big neck muscles, a flint-hard bill, and a long, extensible tongue coated with sticky saliva and tipped with barbs for snagging grubs and insects or slurping sap. Always hungry, young pileated woodpeckers call persistently for food from the nesting cavity; their urgent *wuk-a-wuk-a-wuk-a* echoes through the forest, encouraging the hunting parents. When the young approach full size the adults slow down the delivery of food to encourage them to leave the nest.

The house wren often builds its stick nest in woodpecker holes, but all kinds of cavities have been used — cow skulls, hats, old boots, tin cans, car axles, tea pots, flower pots, abandoned hornet nests, and, of course, bird houses. Unlike other songbirds, which tend to sing most in the early

A young pileated woodpecker calls to its parent from the nest-hole.

morning and evening, the male house wren's clear, bubbling notes are heard all day. An energetic defender of his territory, he tussles on the ground with other males not deterred by his song. Sometimes his vocal persistence attracts two females, and he will mate with both, fathering two broods simultaneously. Although harried by the food demands of his own young, he may find time to puncture the eggs or kill the nestlings of house wrens in neighbouring territories.

A male house wren sings from a prominent perch. Bird song is an important part of territory formation and courtship.

105

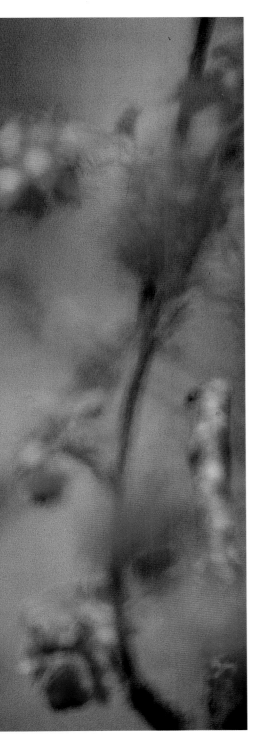

Hummingbirds are the smallest of North American birds. In addition to amazing flying abilities, all have long, tubular bills for syphoning nectar from flowers. In most species the plumage is predominantly iridescent green, and the males have a great variety of brilliantly coloured throat feathers, which they flash during territorial displays. All but one of the more than a dozen North American species are found in the west.

In the courtship of some species, the male flies a pendulum course through the sky above its territory, the mellow tones of its humming wings rising and falling with each swooping change in direction. As if on a string it swings back and forth, up and down, at speeds up to ninety kilometres (fifty-five miles) per hour. At times it plunges straight toward the earth, stopping abruptly a few feet from death, and then shoots off through the forest at a speed the eye cannot follow. It can fly straight up, backwards and sideways, and hover with absolute stillness. Hummingbirds are great long-distance flyers also. The rubythroated, the only hummingbird east of the great plains, migrates across the Gulf of Mexico, a non-stop journey of over 900 kilometres (550 miles).

A male rufous hummingbird perches on a red-flowered currant bush; its blooms produce nectar preferred by hummingbirds.

A female rufous hummingbird hovers motionless; it can fly forward, backward, sideways, or straight up and down, and start and stop with incredible abruptness.

Wherever there is wilderness, the mellow, drawn-out croak of the raven is likely to punctuate the steady whisper of tumbling water and swaying forest. The raven is most common in the western mountains, the Arctic, and the huge boreal forest zone of Canada's north. It is easily distinguished from its close relatives, the crows, even at a distance, when the larger size of the raven is indiscernable. The wedge-shaped tail, shaggy throat, heavily bristled nostrils, and thick, arched bill are its best field marks. In flight the raven is magnificent, alternately flapping and soaring, hovering, diving, and, in courtship, flying wingtip to wingtip and tumble-plunging. It is mainly a scavenger and competes with gulls and vultures for carrion.

A flying raven is readily distinguished by its wedge-shaped tail.

A common raven pulls at a grizzly's salmon catch.

The great grey owl sits motionless and silent on a branch, its glowing yellow eyes directed towards an expanse of fresh snow. The facial discs collect sounds undetectable to the human ear — the vibrations of a mouse tunnelling under the snow. Suddenly the owl drops from the perch, plunging talons first into the thick white cushion. Seconds later, the hunter flies back to its perch to swallow its catch. A few hours after the owl has fed, the indigestible fur and bones are compacted into golf-ball-sized pellets and regurgitated. Owls can often be found by searching for their roosting trees, identified by an accumulation of pellets and white droppings on the ground.

The largest North American owl, the great grey inhabits northern and mountain forests interspersed with meadows or bogs. Like many owls, it lays its eggs in the unused nests of other birds or atop broken trunks. As with many birds of prey, the eggs are laid at intervals, which produces a staggered hatching and results in young of different ages and sizes. At each feeding the largest, most aggressive nestlings are fed first. When prey is plentiful all the young are adequately nourished, but in lean years the oldest is favoured, and it may even eat its brothers and sisters to survive.

If there are severe winter food shortages in northern forests, great grey owls invade more southern regions of Canada and the northern United States. Such rare and irregular invasions attract large crowds of birders who are able to study these fearless owls at close range.

A great grey owl hunts mice and voles from a low perch. It relies on acute hearing to locate its prey, hidden under a blanket of snow.

The long-eared owl is one of the most secretive birds of prey. By day it roosts in dense forests or tangled bottomland. If alarmed it stretches out its slender frame, compresses its bark-patterned feathers, erects its head tufts, and is suddenly transformed from owl to broken snag. A night-time hunter, the long-eared owl eats small rodents and perching birds.

In contrast to the long-eared owl, the saw-whet is small, chunky, and without head tufts. It ranges throughout most of the United States and southern Canada, preferring dense woods. It feeds after dark from a low perch on the edge of a meadow, waiting until small rodents, especially white-footed mice, become active before it flutters silently out to attack. Saw-whet owls prefer to nest in woodpecker holes, especially those of the flicker. They are not aggressive even near the nest, and at times are so tame that they can be caught by hand.

Feathers soaked and dishevelled by rain, a saw-whet owl holds a small songbird in its bill.

A long-eared owl finds an inconspicuous day-time roost.

The forests of Canada and the northeastern United States are breeding habitat for the common goldeneye duck. In spring high-speed courtship flights take place above the trees, the female leading her green-headed mate, their wings sounding the loud and distinctive goldeneye whistle.

The hen soon chooses a cavity — usually a large hollow at the top of a broken tree —insulates it with down and feathers, and lays between eight and twelve eggs. After hatching, the ducklings, coaxed by the hen's clucking, leap from the nest, falling up to fifteen metres (fifty feet) as they flap their tiny wings ineffectively. Saved by thick down and the soft forest floor, they bounce unharmed and follow their mother to the closest pond or lake. She tends the ducklings alone throughout the summer, warily leading them to feeding pools and loafing spots on floating logs or small islands.

In spring pairs of common goldeneyes court on woodland ponds. The female lays her eggs in tree cavities.

Following Pages: A common goldeneye hen and her brood of ducklings rest on a driftwood log.

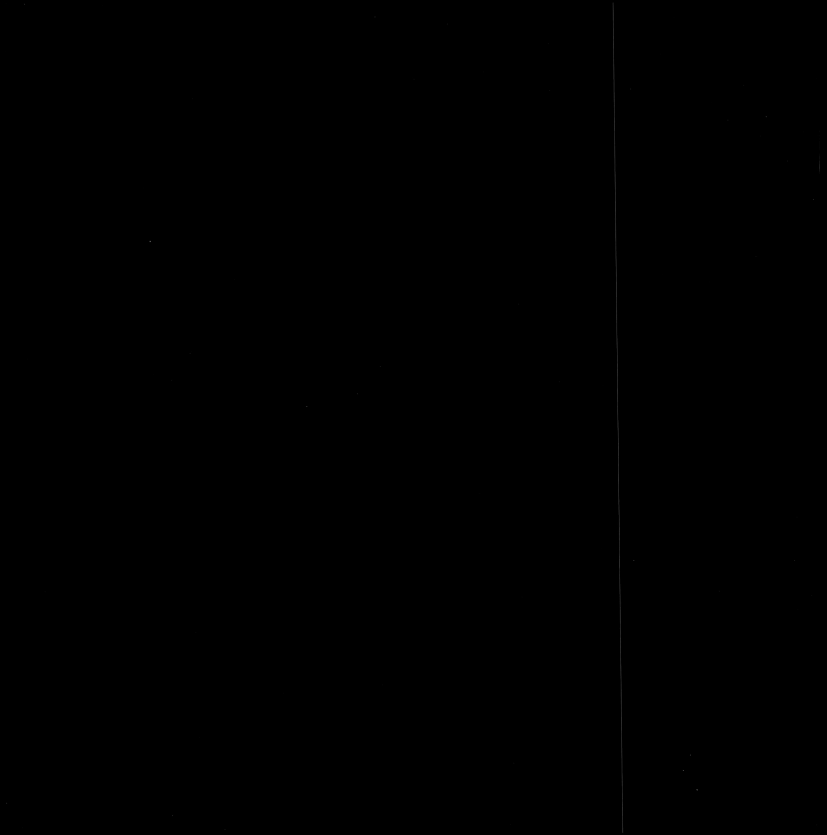

Seashore and Ocean

Seashore and Ocean

Like freshwater species, birds of saltwater habitats are adapted to an aquatic existence: they have dense, oily plumage, webbed feet, and fish-catching beaks. Marine birds have well-developed glands above the nostrils to excrete salt, enabling them to drink sea water when they wander far from land. Long, narrow wings, typical of many seabirds (especially albatrosses) are efficient for gliding, allowing the bird to conserve energy in the absence of resting perches.

Tidal fluctuations create a changing environment for birds of the shoreline. At high tide most species are inactive, returning to feed on invertebrates or fish left exposed and vulnerable at low tide. Crows and gulls crack open shellfish by carrying them aloft and dropping them onto rocks. Diving ducks have powerful gizzards that grind up mussels, shell and all. Small shorebirds called sanderlings feed on invertebrates washed ashore, foraging in lines that rush to and fro with the arrival of each wave.

In an environment without hiding places, many birds have adapted their behaviour to avoid predators. Petrels hunt during the day far out at sea, returning to their nesting islands after dark when they are safe from gulls. Snowy plovers are camouflaged with their sandy habitat, disappearing as soon as they stop moving. When feeding in open tidal flats, dunlin mass together in enormous flocks; if a falcon threatens they swirl up in perfectly synchronized flight that confuses the attacker. Remote, undisturbed islands near food are needed for successful reproduction — habitat so rare that seabirds must breed together in crowded colonies, laying their eggs on ledges, in burrows, or in rock crevices.

Ocean-side birders should consult tide tables in order to synchronize their expeditions with low tide, when many birds are feeding. Birds are also attracted to the abundant food at the mouths of large rivers and areas where there are upswelling currents. More than any other habitat, the open ocean calls for the use of a spotting scope by land-based birders.

A great blue heron glides over a stretch of rocky shoreline on the Pacific coast.

Atlantic puffins rest near their nest burrow on an isolated offshore island.

The Atlantic puffin is a small seabird found off the east coasts of Canada and the northern United States. Its distinctive bill serves many purposes. First, as spring approaches, it grows larger and brighter, making the male more attractive to its mate. Then it becomes a tool for digging out the burrow and amassing nesting material. It is also used for protection (biting), affection (nuzzling), and communication (pointed up it means friendship; pointed down, alarm). The bill holds a dozen or more sardine-sized fish, which the adult airlifts to its hungry chicks in the burrow. By late summer, when the bill begins to shed its outer layers of colour, the breeding grounds become quiet and the colony scatters out over the ocean.

In contrast to the puffin, the cormorant (overleaf) does not endear itself readily to humans. It has a sinister, hawk-like visage, dark, greasy plumage, and a sickly, croaking call; it feeds its young regurgitated fish, and its breeding rookeries are plastered with its own haphazard droppings. But our aesthetic reservations have little to do with the cormorant's adaptative abilities, and numerous closely related species occupy all of North America's coastline except the Arctic.

125

A double-crested cormorant dries its wings in the sun.

The northern gannet winters off the Atlantic and Caribbean coasts of the United States, migrating northwards to breed in six major nesting colonies on islands in the Gulf of St. Lawrence and off Newfoundland. The gannet is a heavy bird, an adaptation that makes it easier to pursue fish underwater, but complicates flight. Even with a wingspan of nearly two metres (seven feet), it has difficulty becoming airborne. Consequently it nests atop seaside cliffs, where it can launch easily into the updraughts. When out fishing, the gannet glides over the swells until it spots prey, then folds its wings and plummets into the sea at over 100 kilometres (60 miles) per hour. In addition to a thick skull, it has inflatable air cells in its neck and breast to cushion the impact.

Gannet colonies seethe with the activity of thousands of birds growling, squabbling, and flying to and from nests often inches apart. They mate for life, maintaining the pair bond by rough and elaborate rituals — neck-biting, bill-fencing, and sky-pointing.

A northern gannet points its bill skyward, a display thought to signal its departure from the nesting colony.

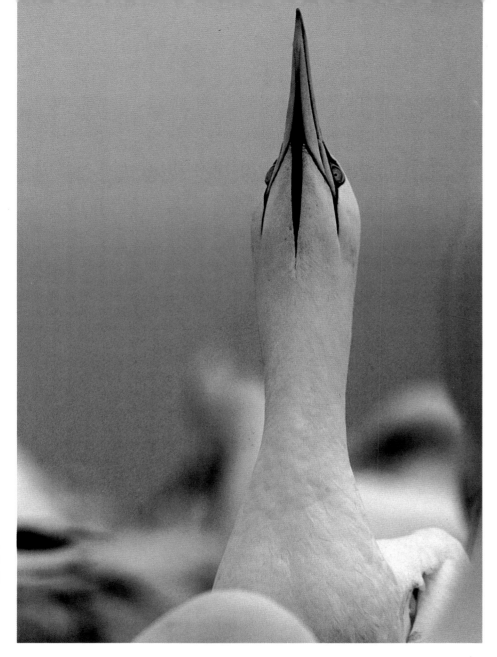

127

Terns and gulls are members of the family *Laridae*, from the Latin word meaning seabird. Terns are easily distinguished from gulls by their pointed bills and wings; most species have white bodies, black caps, and forked tails. Known as 'sea swallows', terns fly on strong, thrusting wings and capture small fish such as herring and minnows, as well as shrimp and squid, by plunge-diving from above. They have weak webbed feet and swim only briefly, hunting predominantly from the air. Reproduction among terns is highest when they are able to nest in dense colonies. They attack intruders vigorously, diving and screaming at them incessantly. Nevertheless, tern colonies suffer the depredations of foxes, rats, raccoons, gulls, and humans. The common tern, one of more than a dozen North American species, is abundant along the east and west coasts and on large inland lakes. Its black-tipped bill distinguishes it from the almost identical Arctic tern.

Gulls are larger and stronger than terns, with heavy, slightly hooked bills. Capable fishers, gulls also scavenge along beaches, docks, and dumps for garbage. At low tide some coastal species gather molluscs and carry them aloft to drop onto rocks, shattering the shells. They are able to drink sea water with the help of glands located above the eyes that eliminate excess salt. Gulls have a variety of calls, which change with each species and with individuals depending on mood and circumstance — from wailing, chuckling, and screaming to shorter notes, some bugle-like, others resembling a hiss or a squeak.

A common tern carries a small fish caught by plunge-diving into the water.

A Bonaparte's gull threatens a rival.

Following Pages: Herring gulls sail along the beach on stiff wings, looking for fish, crabs, and other sea animals cast up by the tide.

131

Three species of mergansers are found in North America. They vary significantly in plumage, size, and distribution. The common merganser is the largest (length 45 cm/18 in.), and males lack the big crest typical of other mergansers. Except for the Arctic, it ranges throughout the continent and is the species most likely to be encountered inland during the winter. The red-breasted merganser is slightly smaller, and the male has a shaggy double crest. It breeds throughout the low Arctic and the boreal forest, and spends the winter along the coasts of southern Canada and the United States. The smallest merganser on the continent is the hooded (length 33 cm/13 in.). It surpasses other mergansers, however, in the beauty of its plumage. The male has a large white crest that opens like a fan during courtship displays. During the nesting season hooded mergansers are found on woodland ponds, rivers, and sheltered backwaters, but many migrate to coastal lagoons and quiet bays for the winter.

A female hooded merganser loafs on a piece of driftwood. Small size distinguishes her from other mergansers.

A hooded merganser drake surfaces with a small fish in its saw-toothed bill.

The black oystercatcher is a crow-sized permanent resident of the Pacific coast, easily recognized by its flattened scarlet bill, yellow eyes, and pink legs. Feeding in the intertidal zone, the oystercatcher uses its long bill to pry limpets from rocks, probe for mussels, and pummel small crabs. When the tide floods the feeding grounds it rests, well-camouflaged among the dark rocks of the shoreline.

The breeding season is a period of dramatic courtship and territorial displays for the oystercatcher. Mates whistle and bow to one another and engage in aerial chases along the shore. The female lays two or three spotted, buffy eggs in the hollow of a rocky islet or on an elevated beach in May or June. The eggs are tended by both sexes, and one month after hatching the young can fly and open shellfish with their bills.

A pair of black oystercatchers parades along a gravel bar.

The sandpiper family is one of the most exciting for birdwatchers. Not only are there many species of similar size and shape, but in the fall the moulting of colourful breeding feathers and the presence of young birds still in nondescript juvenile plumage make it a challenge to distinguish species in mixed flocks. The western sandpiper is the size of a house sparrow and migrates from its Arctic breeding grounds to the coastal United States with other similar sandpipers. Except for its black legs it is easily confused with the least sandpiper, whose legs are greenish-yellow, and except for its longer bill, with the more abundant but almost identical semipalmated sandpiper.

The greater yellowlegs is a large, long-legged, and wary sandpiper, apt to be the first bird in a foraging flock to raise its strident alarm call and take flight. Its pointed bill is used not to probe but rather to pluck up swimming insects and fish, or to skim small prey from the water with a back-and-forth motion. During winter and in migration the greater yellowlegs is one of the most common birds of coastal mud-flats and marshes. Except for size, it is almost identical to its smaller relative the lesser yellowlegs, which is more common in the east and midwest.

When resting on a rocky shoreline, the black turnstone's sepia head, neck, and back render it almost invisible. On the wing, however, its shrill cry and white wing bars, rump, and belly make identification of this sandpiper easy even at a distance. Black turnstones breed in Alaska and spend the winter along the Pacific coast of British Columbia, the United States, and Mexico.

Western sandpipers wait for low tide to expose mud-flats where they can feed.

A greater yellowlegs wades in the shallows, hunting for small fish and other animals.

Following Pages: Flocks of black turnstones are common along the Pacific coast during spring and fall migration, as well as in winter.

Sea ducks are distinguished by their short necks, stout bodies, and ability to dive underwater. Most species breed in the far north and pass the winter along the coast.

Harlequin ducks are easily recognized, the drakes by their flamboyant plumage, the hens by three white spots on both sides of the head. On the coast harlequins feed close to shore, swimming in tight formations over shelves, reefs, and sunken rocks. They use their wings and feet to dive for small crustaceans, molluscs, and occasionally fish. In their breeding streams in the mountains they feed by walking along the gravel bottom, like dippers, keeping low to fight against the current. They poke under rocks for stonefly and mayfly nymphs, caddisfly larvae, and other small animals. The nest of grass and leaves is placed on the ground, under a bush or in a rock crevice. The female's drab plumage keeps her obscure while she incubates. On hatching, the ducklings leave the nest immediately and hide out beneath over-hanging streamside vegetation while they grow to flying stage.

The white-winged scoter is the sea duck most likely to be found inland during the winter. It is most abundant on the coast, however, where it is found in large flocks, usually with other scoters. The white-winged scoter eats almost any kind of marine life it can find, but subsists mostly on molluscs, especially blue mussels, which it tears from the bottom with its strong bill, swallows whole, and grinds up in its powerful gizzard. Scoters shot by hunters have been found with hundreds of small mussels in their stomachs. Scoters move up and down the coast in long undulating lines, flying fast and low over the swells. White-winged scoters are easily told from other scoter species by their white wing patches, which flash in flight.

As its name implies, the harlequin drake is one of the most brightly coloured sea ducks.

White-winged scoters rest on the surface between feeding dives.

The belted kingfisher is found on lakes and rivers throughout North America except in the arctic tundra. In coastal regions it inhabits salt marshes, estuaries, and lagoons, where it perches on a piling or an overhanging snag, its oversized shaggy head and dagger beak angled studiously downward as it watches for prey. Sometimes it reconnoitres the shoreline, hovering momentarily and then moving on until it captures a fish or crab. Then the bird returns to shore to bludgeon the prize against the perch and mince it thoroughly in its heavy beak before swallowing it.

Kingfishers defend their territories vigorously, especially during the nesting season. They swoop on the heels of other kingfishers, chasing them angrily through mazes of trees or wharf pilings at top speed, driving the intruders off with rattling alarm calls. Using their sturdy bills and feet like pickaxes and shovels, kingfishers dig out nest burrows up to three metres (ten feet) long in sandy bluffs, where they lay four to six eggs.

A belted kingfisher hunts a tide pool from a Douglas-fir snag.

149

There are five members of the ibis family in North America. The most common species is the white ibis; the largest is the roseate spoonbill. Both are found in southern coastal mangrove swamps and marshes. Ibises are medium to large size birds with long bills, long legs, short tails, and partial webbing of the toes. They are usually found in flocks. When airborne, they fly with heads extended and legs trailing, and alternate between flapping and gliding. Airborne flocks usually form long undulating lines, sometimes a V.

The white ibis has a long, thin, down-curved bill which it uses to probe the mud for crabs or pluck insects from the grass. It is likely to be seen feeding among the arching roots of mangroves at low tide. In flight its black wing tips and snow white body make it easy to distinguish. Immature birds have brownish heads and upperparts.

The roseate spoonbill is unmistakable with its spatula shaped bill, white and pink body, orange tail, naked pale green head, and scarlet eyes and legs. It forages the coastal shallows, sweeping its bill through the water. Nerves lining the bill are sensitive to small aquatic animals such as crabs, worms, fish, frogs, molluscs, and insects, and signal the bill to snap shut when prey is encountered. The spoonbill punctuates its feeding with grunts and gobbling sounds.

A white ibis pauses momentarily in its search for prey.

A roseate spoonbill issues its guttural call.

151

Desert and Scrubland

Desert and Scrubland

This world of cactus and thornbush, of rock gulches and persistent blue skies, is a mecca for birdwatchers. Desert birdlife is abundant, varied, and peppered with interesting species. The open terrain and clear atmosphere provide wide-ranging views and easy spotting.

North America's deserts cover vast areas of the West. Best known is the Sonoran Desert of Arizona and southwestern California, where giant saguaros tower several storeys over smaller cacti, thorn trees, and wildflowers. The other desert regions — Mojave, Great Basin, and Chihuahuan — though not so dramatic, are nevertheless home to many species unique to such arid habitats.

Desert birds are adapted to survive not only dryness but extremes of heat and cold. Many species have light-coloured plumage that reflects the sun's heat and also provides camouflage. Some birds shed excess body heat by increasing blood circulation through bare-skinned legs. Others re-absorb moisture from their urine, excreting nearly solid waste. Roadrunners and common nighthawks can hibernate briefly during frosty nights or sweltering days, saving the energy needed to maintain a constant body temperature.

Look for birds in the morning and evening, when it is cooler. During midday, most species disappear into shaded areas, perching in shrubs above the hot ground. Heat drives the burrowing owl underground and forces hole-nesting species, like the gila woodpecker, ash-throated flycatcher, and elf owl, into the insulated cavities of cacti. The starlit nights of the desert are ideal for watching owls, which are easily located by playing tapes of their calls. Most owls will answer and fly closer to the source of the recording.

Aside from coordinating your field trips with the activity of the birds, search areas close to water holes, streams, and washes (even if they appear dry) where birds come regularly to drink. Wear sturdy shoes to protect against stabbing cacti and sharp rocks, drink water regularly to avoid dehydration, and wear a hat to ward off sunstroke.

A turkey vulture soars above the arid terrain of Monument Valley, Arizona.

Golden eagles mate for life. During courtship the male and female engage in spectacular flight maneuvers and displays, sometimes touching wings as they spiral upward or nose-dive through the air at speeds over 160 kilometers (100 miles) per hour. They build huge stick nests three metres (ten feet) across and one metre (three feet) deep on high cliffs or in trees. The eaglets, usually two, hatch several days apart. The youngest is attacked and often killed by its bigger sibling, a matter that seems of no concern to the parents.

The young are fed pieces of small mammals, birds, and snakes until they are strong enough to rip the prey apart on their own. At ten weeks the young eagles' dark juvenile plumage is complete and they are ready to fly, although they remain dependent on their parents for at least another month.

A golden eagle offers food to its nestling.

The roadrunner got its name in earlier times from running down roads ahead of horsedrawn vehicles. It is actually a giant cuckoo, almost two feet long, that seldom flies. Like all cuckoos, its large toes form an X with two toes pointing forward and two backward. Combined with long legs, they enable the roadrunner to reach speeds of twenty-four kilometers (fifteen miles) per hour in pursuit of insects, lizards, small rodents, and snakes. Roadrunners establish a permanent pair bond and live in their territory year-round.

During courtship, listen for the male's low, plaintive cooing and watch for his bowing and fanning displays. The female lays three to five eggs in a shallow nest in a low shrub or cactus. The young hatch at intervals, and if food becomes scarce, the largest seizes all that the parents bring, leaving the smaller ones to starve.

A greater roadrunner searches the desert floor for food. When cold, it exposes a dark patch of feathers on its back to absorb sunlight.

159

The northern cardinal is an adaptable species whose range extends over much of the eastern United States and into the desert areas of the Southwest. It is named after the cardinals of the Roman Catholic Church whose robes, like the plumage of the male bird, are scarlet. The female is olive grey with reddish wings and crest. One of America's best loved songbirds, the cardinal feeds and nests in small trees, thickets, and hedge rows.

A relative of the northern cardinal, the pyrrhuloxia has the same distinctive red crest but greyer plumage, and a yellow, down-curved bill. The duller plumage provides good camouflage in the dry, thorny thickets and mesquite forests of the Southwest, where it is a permanent resident. During courtship, only the flamboyant males sing the whistled, cardinal-like songs. Aggressive defenders of territory, males are gentle in their courtship rituals, passing sunflower seeds to the female of their choice. Like the cardinal, the pyrrhuloxia is a faithful visitor to desert birdfeeders.

A cardinal cracks open a sunflower seed with its heavy bill.

A male pyrrhuloxia perches on the branch of a mesquite tree.

The prairie falcon is one of the swiftest birds of prey. With a streamlined torso, bullet-like head, short thick neck, powerful shoulders, and long pointed wings, it is well suited for the dashing maneuvers that characterize its hunting behaviour. Much of its diet consists of birds, some of which are overtaken in direct low-level flight. Small birds, like its favourite target the horned lark, are simply plucked out of the air. The falcon captures others by diving swiftly from above and knocking them to the ground with a blow from its large talons.

During the spring, the prairie falcon remains near its nesting site, usually a shallow depression scraped out of the soil or loose gravel of a decomposing rock ledge. The use of pesticides and the spread of agriculture have caused a serious decline in falcon numbers.

A prairie falcon launches from a guano-spattered cliff.

The richly coloured Harris hawk is easily recognized by reddish shoulders, wing linings, and thighs, and a white, terminal tail band and rump. It is common along the coastal prairies of southern Texas and the arid scrubland along the Mexican border. Often Harris hawks nest in the crotch of a tall saguaro cactus. Sometimes a trio of two males and a female nest together; the extra male helps feed the chicks and bring food to the nest.

Harris hawks also hunt in teams. Sometimes five to six birds (a breeding pair, unmated adults, and immatures from the previous season) surround a thicket sheltering desert cottontails and jackrabbits. One hawk swoops over the thicket to scare prey into the open, where the others are waiting to strike. They share the kill, an unusual habit for raptors which normally guard their food from all but their mates.

A Harris hawk leaves its nest in a saguaro cactus with a partially eaten bird.

While brooding its young, a Harris hawk keeps a look-out for its mate.

Thrashers are large members of the mocking-bird family. They are not strong fliers, preferring to run along the ground and use their strong bills to dig for insects and worms. Their noticeably short wings and long tails, legs, and bills are adaptations to these terrestrial habits.

The sage thrasher, smallest of eight North American thrasher species, is a characteristic bird of western sagebrush plains. Nondescript in appearance, its song is arresting — a melodic, extended series of warbled phrases. The larger curve-billed thrasher is common in dry canyons and brushlands. It is at home in cactus country, landing with impunity on a cholla or teddy bear cactus bristling with spines.

A sage thrasher stands poised on a prairie boulder, ready to broadcast its spring song.

A curve-billed thrasher perches on a prickly pear cactus.

Great Birding Spots

Great Birding Spots

The places described in this chapter are intended for the beginning birdwatcher. In all of these locations, there will be plenty of birds in plain view, but generally only during certain periods of the year. Many species will be easy to identify; others will have you buried in your field guide. In addition to being a rich environment for birds, these locations offer other exciting wildlife or scenic attractions.

To get the most enjoyment from a birding excursion, you need to schedule your trip to catch the birds during their most active period — usually during breeding or migration. Regional bird guides are inexpensive and generally provide the most specific and up-to-date information. You can purchase these at gift shops in National Parks, at National Wildlife Refuge visitor centres, and in local bookstores once you have reached your destination.

Southeastern Arizona

My favourite birding area in the United States, the dry, hot, and rugged region of southeastern Arizona offers many attractions aside from an agreeable climate. The most unique is the Sonoran desert, a magical habitat of giant saguaro, cholla, prickly pear, and many other cacti, ocotillo and sagebrush, mesquite and palo verde trees, and wildflowers in early spring. Here the birds are strong-voiced, easily spotted, and abundant. The desert areas are spread among various mountain ranges, which produce a variety of other habitats: shaded river canyons lined with sycamores, oaks, and cottonwoods; foothills covered with pinon pine and juniper; and mountainsides where ponderosa pine and Douglas-fir project from lingering snowpacks. These vegetation zones are mostly dependent on elevation, and as a result it is possible to pass through several zones in a few minutes of driving.

Birdwatchers at High Island, Texas scan the tree canopy for migrants.

This variety of habitats is matched by a diversity of birds. Many species are only found in the Southwest. Local desert specialties are the roadrunner, cactus wren, Harris hawk, white-winged dove, pyrrhuloxia, curve-billed thrasher, gila woodpecker, and Gambel's quail. In the mountains (the Chiricahua range is best), you will encounter new species of birds whenever you gain or lose elevation: brown towhees and acorn woodpeckers in the foothills, black-headed grosbeaks and western tanagers at mid-elevation, and mountain chickadees and Steller's jays at the summit — to cite a few examples.

Of special appeal are the many canyons scattered through southeastern Arizona. Due to localized conditions of moisture, elevation, and sun exposure, each canyon has its own special blend of plants and birds. You will want to visit Sabino Canyon, Madera Canyon, and Ramsey Canyon.

Southeastern Arizona is the hummingbird capital of the United States, with more than a dozen species. There are hummer resorts where humans have set up feeders which attract hundreds of birds everyday. Any time is good, but late summer rains bring out the wildflowers and bring in the hummingbirds.

Access: Make Tucson your headquarters, especially if you are flying. There are plenty of restaurants, motels, gas stations, and campgrounds throughout the region. Time your visit for early May, when bird activity is peaking, a few wildflowers are still blooming, and midday temperatures are not yet extreme. Southeastern Arizona is popular with birders, and you will meet many people with whom you will be able to share information.

Other Attractions: The Arizona-Sonora Desert Museum (west of Tucson) is a world famous zoo exhibiting only local wildlife and plants in natural, open air settings. Saguaro National Monument is a sanctuary for giant saguaro cacti and a great place for birding. Ramsey Mile-Hi Ranch is renowned for hummingbirds attracted to feeders. The Sonoita Creek Sanctuary is an endangered riparian tract protected by the Nature Conservancy.

The Everglades, Florida

Found at the southern tip of Florida, the Everglades is an extensive, flat, low-lying, sub-tropical region of diverse habitat, most of which lies within Everglades National Park (14 million acres). Birdlife is more abundant here than anywhere else on the continent.

Most of the land is overgrown with sawgrass and looks like African savannah, an impression that dissipates quickly should you step from the trail into the

A Costa's hummingbird rests briefly from feeding on desert wildflowers.

White-winged doves perch on a decaying saguaro cactus in the Sonoran Desert.

muck hidden by the tall grass. You will see ospreys, bald eagles, and most of North America's herons and ibises in this habitat, as well as such Everglade specialties as the limpkin and Everglades kite.

Scattered through these marshes are humps of land (called hammocks) covered with stunted trees of tropical origin — gumbo-limbo, tamarind, papaya, strangler fig. These jungle-like confines are home to barred owls, red-shouldered hawks, white-crowned pigeons, various warblers, and other passerine species.

Near the sea, the sawgrass gives way to mangrove swamps. These scrubby entanglements are nesting habitat for thousands of wading birds, pelicans, cormorants, and anhingas. Along the coast, in the shallow, pale blue waters of Florida Bay, you will encounter American oystercatchers, roseate spoonbills, reddish egrets, black skimmers, great white herons, and a diversity of gulls, terns, and sandpipers.

Access: Miami is the main urban centre located about one hour northeast of the Everglades. Make your first stop at the National Park visitors' facility. There are campgrounds and a lodge within the park, but it is necessary to make reservations. Motel accommodations at Homestead, just outside the park, are limited. The same goes for service stations and restaurants. Your first visit should be during February

or March, when the dry season forces birds to concentrate in gator holes and ponds.

Other Attractions: There is great birding all the way to Key West. The two-lane highway leapfrogs its way for more than a hundred miles over scores of beautiful islands and coves, and, unfortunately, runaway commercial development. Ding Darling National Wildlife Refuge on Sanibel Island is a winter haven for waterfowl and a great place for canoeing. Famed Corkscrew Swamp, an Audubon sanctuary that protects a stand of giant baldcypress, is a nesting site for hundreds of endangered woodstorks.

Bonaventure Island, Quebec

A small, uninhabited island off the tip of Quebec's Gaspé Peninsula, Bonaventure is site of the most accessible and spectacular seabird colonies in North America. During the summer, tens of thousands of northern gannets, along with smaller numbers of Atlantic puffins, razorbills, common murres, black-legged kittiwakes, black guillemots, and various gull species form breeding colonies on the rocky seaward-facing cliffs.

To reach Bonaventure Island, located

In the Florida Everglades, a limpkin has pulled a mussel from the bottom.

Razorbills gather at the base of Percé Rock.

warblers, hermit thrushes, fox sparrows, purple finches, and pine siskins. Brush up on the songs of these birds before your hike, and try sorting out these species on your hike into their colonies.

The gannets are packed nearly shoulder to shoulder along the upper cliffs, spilling over onto the grassy knoll on top. A fence keeps observers from approaching the colony too closely, but in good years the birds spread beyond it. Breeding rituals, incubation, feeding the young, and the social organization of the colony can be studied at leisure, as can the gannet's spectacular fishing methods, which occur at the food of the cliffs. It is a noisy scene of non-stop action.

Access: Plan your visit for June or July. The closest airport is in Quebec City some 650 kilometres (400 miles) away. Your approach by car follows the St. Lawrence River and the Gulf coastline the entire way, a scenic route that passes through many French villages. There are good motels, restaurants, and campgrounds in Percé, but make reservations in advance.

Other Attractions: This region is covered with northern spruce forests, a hotspot for nesting warblers and other songbirds. Be sure to walk out to Perce Rock at low tide, where you will be rewarded with not only close views of this famous geologic formation, but guillemots, kittiwakes, gulls,

three kilometres (two miles) offshore, you must take one of the frequent ferries from the quaint French Canadian village of Percé. The boat circles the Island before landing to give visitors an ocean-level view of the seventy-five-metre (250-foot) cliffs where the birds nest. The trail across the island to the rookeries winds through balsam fir and spruce woods alive with breeding songbirds — Tennessee warblers, black-throated green warblers, magnolia

176

and razorbills nesting in the cluttered rocks at the base of the cliff.

Cape May, New Jersey

Over the years, this has been the hottest birding spot in North America. Shaped like a giant funnel, Cape May collects migrants moving south along the Atlantic flyway and concentrates them at the tip, where there are usually plenty of bird-watchers lying in wait. Here, birds are suddenly confronted with a great gap in the coastline — Delaware Bay, a thirty kilometre (eighteen mile) stretch of open water. They must fly across nonstop, or retreat inland to a longer but safer route. Some continue without hesitation. Others loaf about the shoreline, gathering energy or waiting for favourable winds. A strong northwest wind can blow the birds help-lessly out to sea, and consequently causes great numbers to pile up at the end of the Cape until the weather changes.

Cape May offers interesting birding at any time, with good numbers and variety, but the last half of the year is best. Exceptional aggregations of species begin in August, when tree swallows seem to be swirling everywhere. Their numbers build steadily as they are joined by other swallow species. Later in the month, the first wave of a flood of eastern kingbirds washes over the suburban neighborhoods of the Cape.

Next to make their presence obvious are bobolinks in their reedy winter plumage. They are accompanied by the first raptors — ospreys and American kestrels, most of them hatched out the previous spring. Throughout September, there is a steady trickle of northern flickers, which some-times increases to a stream of fifty birds per minute passing over a single vantage point. (Pick any high dune along the beach.) October is the best month for hawks, especially soaring hawks (buteos), but also sharp-shinned, Cooper's, and a few pere-grine falcons and merlins. The tide of migrants subsides in November with a final gush of American woodcocks, usually hiding out during the day in thickets and hedgerows back from the dunes.

There are, of course, scores of other species to be found in woodlots, meadows, and suburban gardens, not to mention seashore and ocean habitats. Although the presence of humans is felt everywhere on Cape May, it remains a premier birding area. Even in winter, when migration has subsided, there are more than 130 species found here.

Access: If you are flying, Philadelphia is the closest major center. The best birdwatch-ing occurs in September and October. There are many restaurants, motels, and gas stations.

Other Attractions: Although heavily pop-ulated, there is much woodland, salt marsh, and coastal habitat to be explored. Brigan-tine National Wildlife Refuge protects about 20,000 acres of prime waterfowl breeding habitat. It is also a great spot for herons, rails, and shorebirds of many species.

Churchill/Hudson Bay, Manitoba

The most easily accessible arctic birding is found in Churchill, Manitoba — a small, remote town on the shores of Hudson Bay, established as a port for shipping grain. Situated on the treeline, it allows the birder to walk in a few minutes from the quiet precincts of a stunted spruce grove into open permafrost tundra strewn with rocks and boulders and cushioned elsewhere with sedges, grasses, and lichens. Many of the birds you may have seen migrating through your neighborhood back home, but this is their breeding grounds, and their be-haviour and appearance will be strikingly different.

Of Churchill's varied habitats, the most renowned among naturalists is the tundra, a hotspot for observing nesting shorebirds. In mid-June, amidst an explosion of wild-flowers, you can witness whimbrel, lesser golden-plover, least sandpiper, red-necked phalarope, Hudsonian godwit, and others in rich breeding plumage, full song, and ritualized display.

177

In addition to shorebirds, the tundra is the breeding site for hoary redpoll, short-eared owl, lapland longspur, northern shrike, willow ptarmigan, and snow bunting. The boreal forests harbour grey jay, orange-crowned and blackpoll warblers, American tree sparrow, pine grosbeak, and (less commonly) spruce grouse, boreal owl, and bohemian waxwing. Northern serenades emanate from areas of marsh and muskeg — the gulping thunder of American bitterns, the winnowing sounds of diving snipe, the jangling flight call of lesser yellowlegs, and the haunting yodel of Pacific loons.

Where the Churchill River enters the immense expanse of Hudson Bay, you will see arctic terns and parasitic jaegers feeding on the fish stirred up by pods of beluga whales that congregate here. Other water-birds in evidence among the broken ice-floes include red-breasted merganser, king eider, harlequin duck, and Sabine's gull.

Access: The best time to visit is mid-June. You can fly into Churchill from Winnipeg, or you can take one of the last great wilderness train rides in North America from Thompson, Manitoba. Churchill has ample motels and restaurants. You can

Waterfowl, like this mallard drake, and shorebirds are common in the tidal habitat at Cape May.

178

The willow ptarmigan is likely to be encountered in the tundra habitats surrounding Churchill, Manitoba.

Black-necked stilts mate in a wet meadow. They are common in the Klamath Basin.

rent a car or pick-up truck from one of the residents, or even hire a local person to take you birdwatching. There are only a few miles of roads leading out of town. Much of the area is accessible by foot. You will bump into many birdwatchers, naturalists, and field researchers.

Other Attractions: Churchill is a frontier town, and you will enjoy visiting the general store, talking to the residents, many of whom are natives, and strolling about the delapidated buildings. Visit the ruins of Fort Pierce, built by the Hudson Bay Company in the 1700s, and the polar

bear jail, which may have an inmate or two even though most bears do not show up around town until early fall.

Klamath Basin, California

Lying at the foot of the Cascade Mountains in southern Oregon and northern California, the Klamath Basin is world-renowned for its autumn concentrations of waterfowl — millions of ducks, geese, and swans pass through in migration. Funneling southward from breeding grounds as remote as Siberia, undulating flocks can darken the skies in October. The visitor may see, in a single glance, as many as 250,000 snow geese rising *en masse* against the snowcapped eminence of Mount Shasta. In all, more than 275 species have been sighted here, including 180 nesting species. Bald eagles are more abundant here than any place outside Alaska, with more than 500 spending the winter feeding on sick and injured waterfowl.

Much of the prime marsh habitat has been lost to agricultural development, but tens of thousands of acres receive some measure of protection, most notably in four national wildlife refuges, each offering distinctive attractions for the bird lover. The Oregon unit (Upper Klamath NWR) is mostly open water and cattail and tule marsh, accessible only by boat. Canoes can be rented, and there is a trail that leads

birders through habitat frequented by grebes, herons, pelicans, rails, coots, shore-birds, and others.

The California units are more diverse and easily viewed by foot and by car. Lower Klamath Refuge hosts the largest number of breeding waterfowl; Clear Lake Refuge is dotted with small islands where white pelicans, double-crested cormorants, Caspian terns, and various gulls have established nesting colonies. On the surrounding sagebrush uplands, sage grouse strut about their courtship arenas in late March and April. Other semi-desert specialties breed here, including four sparrows — the vesper, lark, Brewer's, and sage sparrows — that will challenge your identification skills.

The Tule Lake Refuge is best known for its hundreds of nesting western, eared, and pied-billed grebes. All of the National Wildlife Refuge units are administered from Tule Lake Headquarters in Tule Lake, where maps and information are available.

Access: Major cities (Sacramento and Port-land) are about 500 kilometres (300 miles) distant. Klamath Falls, forty kilometres (twenty-five miles) to the north is the

Hundreds of thousands of snow geese gather in the Klamath Basin during migration.

closest large town. Tule Lake, eight kilometres (five miles) east of the refuge headquarters, has limited motels, gas, and restaurants.

Other Attractions: Much of the area is typical western sagebrush country, with abundant coyote and mule deer that are most likely seen at dawn and dusk. Crater Lake National Park is 120 kilometres (seventy-five miles) to the northwest. Its central feature is a 2500-metre (8000-foot) volcano called Mount Mazama, whose towering, jagged peaks surround the calm waters of Crater Lake, the deepest lake in the United States.

Point Pelee, Ontario

This flat spit of land, projecting southward into Lake Erie for fifteen kilometres (nine miles) has long been a mecca for birdwatchers. It is thought by many birders to provide the most dramatic show of migrating species anywhere on the continent. Most of the area is preserved inside Point Pelee National Park.

One of the best times to visit is May, and if bad weather descends on Point Pelee from the north, there will be an exciting "fall-out" of birds. Crossing Lake Erie into the wind, northbound migrants make for Point Pelee, the nearest landfall. Arriving exhausted and unwary, they are scrutinized by eager scope and binocular-wielding birders from all over the world. During a storm in mid-May, the peninsula will be alive with tanagers, flycatchers, orioles, vireos, grosbeaks, buntings, thrushes, swallows, and especially warblers.

Even though Point Pelee is small and isolated amidst heavy agricultural and suburban development, it is more than just a turnstile for migrants. Its varied habitats — mature hardwood forest, cattail marshes, overgrown fields and orchards, brush, beach dunes, ponds, and of course, open lake — meet the reproductive and feeding requirements of many species. Convenient access into the marsh is provided by nearly a mile of boardwalk, which leads to an observation tower. More than 330 bird species have been recorded at Pelee.

Access: The cities of Windsor and Detroit are less than an hour's drive to the west. There are ample lodgings, restaurants, and gas stations in the area. If you wish to meet other birdwatchers (always a good idea), stay at the Pelee Motor Inn just outside the park.

Other Attractions: Point Pelee is also known for migrants other than birds,

---

Songbirds, like this yellow-rumped warbler, arrive at Point Pelee exhausted from flying across Lake Erie.

including dragonflies, monarch butterflies, and bats. Hawk Cliff Sanctuary, also on the north shore of Lake Erie east of Point Pelee, offers great views of migrating raptors in the fall. Jack Miner's Bird Sanctuary is a staging area for large numbers of geese and waterfowl best seen in late March/early April and late October/early November. Long Point, also on Lake Erie, is a well-known waterfowl staging area and home of North America's first bird observatory. It has an active bird-banding program, and welcomes visitors and volunteer helpers.

Platte River, Nebraska

Each year at winter's end, Nebraska's central Platte River Valley comes alive with the impressive sights and sounds of

the largest gathering of any crane species in the world. Some 200,000 sandhill cranes, migrating from wintering areas in New Mexico and Texas, convene here for a month or so to feed and rest.

These tall, long-legged birds, with their resounding, gargling calls, are drawn to the Platte for several reasons. The river satisfies the cranes' special requirements for a night roost — a broad, shallow river channel (600 metres/2000 feet wide and less than fifteen centimetres/six inches deep) whose islands and sandbars are free of vegetation. There is also abundant food in the surrounding countryside. The cranes probe the wet meadows near the river for tubers, worms, insects, frogs, and snakes emerging from hibernation. They fly further afield to forage cultivated fields for waste grain. Biologists believe this rich diet is essential to fortify the cranes for the long trek north and the subsequent stress of reproduction.

There are only 128 kiliometres (eighty miles) of the Platte River where good numbers of cranes can be found. The longest stretch is between Grand Island and Lexington; another is between North

---

Preceding Page: Sandhill cranes perform their characteristic dance. Thousands of these cranes stage along the Platte River during migration.

Platte and Sutherland. There are few cranes elsewhere. Once, most of the Platte was sandhill crane habitat, but the water has been diverted for irrigation, causing the channels to narrow and vegetation to grow on sandbars and islands.

Access: Plan your visit for mid-March. Lincoln, Nebraska is the closest approach by air. Crane viewing headquarters is in Kearney, 240 kilometres (150 miles) away, where there is much excitement and information about the cranes during migration. Ample services are available. Be sure to take winter clothing.

Other Attractions: The Rainwater Basin south of Kearney is intensively farmed, but more than forty waterfowl refuges are scattered through the area. Many species migrate through this area during March, including ninety percent of the mid-continent population of white-fronted geese.

Other wildlife — bald eagles, ducks, geese, whooping cranes, songbirds, deer, mink, muskrat, and beaver — all use the Platte as a migratory resting spot or as a permanent home.

Texas Coast

The Texas Coast offers perhaps the widest range of birding experiences of any location in the United States. Much of the shoreline is comprised of marshes, shallow lagoons,

sandbars, and mangrove swamps that attract a great number and variety of wading birds and over-wintering grebes, loons, waterfowl, and shorebirds. Of particular renown is Aransas National Wildlife Refuge where endangered whooping cranes pass the winter. The best way to view these large waders is to board one of the birding tour boats, which leave several times daily from the town of Rockport.

Birds migrating to and from South and Central America pass along the Texas coast during fall and spring. Nowhere can one get a better view of migrating songbirds than in the little town of High Island, located about forty kilometres (twenty-five miles) north of Galveston. This slight hump in an otherwise table-flat landscape is the only place for miles where there are trees. Warblers, vireos, thrushes, grosbeaks, buntings, and orioles, exhausted by their flight across the Gulf of Mexico, home in on this solitary refuge. The best time to visit is during stormy weather in mid-April, when the oak and hackberry trees are alive with these songbirds in brilliant breeding plumage.

While you are in the High Island vicinity, be sure to visit Bolivar Flats at low

An Attwater's prairie-chicken displays on its courtship ground in Texas.

tide, to see perhaps the most varied aggregation of shorebirds on the continent (including avocets in flocks of a thousand) and hundreds of white and brown pelicans loafing on the sandbars. It is an excellent spot to see and compare as many as thirty species of shorebirds at once.

Another attraction for birders is in Texas' deep south, along the Rio Grande River. Here, sub-tropical vegetation draws rarities from Mexico, including the least grebe, black-bellied whistling tree duck, chachalaca, tropical kingbird, kiskadee flycatcher, and the hook-billed kite. Don't miss the tiny but spectacular Santa Ana National Wildlife Refuge, one of the best places to experience this habitat.

Access: Fly or drive into Houston. Abundant facilities are available along the length of the coast. April is the best time to visit.

Other Attractions: The Attwater Prairie Chicken Refuge west of Houston is home to this endangered sub-species. They perform their courtship dances during March and April. The Texas Hill Country west of Austin and San Antonio is ablaze with wildflowers during April, although you will see plenty of beautiful patches elsewhere.

Brown pelicans, black skimmers, and laughing gulls loaf on a Texas sandbar.

Suggested Reading

Field Guides

Cornell Laboratory of Ornithology. *The Peterson Field Guide Series: A Field Guide to Bird Songs of Eastern and Central America*, 2nd ed. 2 cassette tapes. Boston: Houghton Mifflin Co., 1983.

Cornell Laboratory of Ornithology. *The Peterson Field Guide to Western Bird Songs: A Field Guide to Western Bird Songs: Western North America and the Hawaiian Islands*. 3 cassette tapes. Boston: Houghton Mifflin Co., 1975.

Elliot, L. *Know Your Bird Songs*. vol. I & II. 2 cassette tapes. Ithaca, New York: Nature Sound Studio, 1991.

Farrand, J. Jr., ed. *The Audubon Master Guide to Birding*. 3 vols. New York: Alfred A. Knopf, 1983.

Robbins, C.S., B. Bruun, and H.S. Zim. *Birds of North America: A Guide to Field Identification*, revised ed. New York: Golden Press, 1983.

Scott, S.L., ed. *Field Guide to the Birds of North America*. 2nd ed. Washington, D.C.: National Geographic Society, 1987.

Birdwatching

Connor, J. *The Complete Birder: A Guide to Better Birding*. Boston: Houghton Mifflin Co., 1988.

Finley, J.C. ed. *A Bird-Finding Guide to Canada*. Edmonton: Hurtig Publishers Ltd., 1984.

Pettingill, O.S. Jr. *A Guide to Bird Finding East of the Mississippi*, 2nd ed. New York: Oxford University Press, 1977.

Pettingill, O.S. Jr. *A Guide to Bird Finding West of the Mississippi*, 2nd ed. New York: Oxford University Press, 1981.

Riley, L. and W. *Guide to the National Wildlife Refuges*. Garden City, New York: Anchor Books, 1981.

Bird Biology

Bent, A.C. *Life Histories of North American Birds*. 20 vol. series. New York: Dover Publications, 1963.

Ehrlich, P., D.S. Dobkin and D. Wheye. *The Birder's Handbook*. New York: Simon and Shuster, Inc., 1988.

Stokes, D.W. *A Guide to Bird Behavior*, vol. I. Boston, Toronto: Little, Brown and Co., 1979.

Stokes, D.W. and Stokes, L.Q. *A Guide to Bird Behavior*, vol. II & III. Boston, Toronto: Little, Brown and Co., 1983, 1989.

Terres, J.K. *The Audubon Society Encyclopedia of North American Birds*. New York: Alfred A. Knopf, 1980.

Van Tyne, J., and Berger, A.J. *Fundamentals of Ornithology*. New York: John Wiley and Sons, 1976.

Index of Plates

PRODUCED BY TERRAPIN BOOKS

Project Director: Audrey Fraggalosch
Consulting Editors: Sally Livingston, Greg Linder
Book Design: Sean O'Malley, Kristal Metz
Typography: Marcus Yearout, Janice Wisman
Graphic Assembly: Rod Burton, Vivian Reece
Art Consultant: Susan Bennerstrom
Production: Dan Joyce